A GIFT FOR:

....

FROM:

....

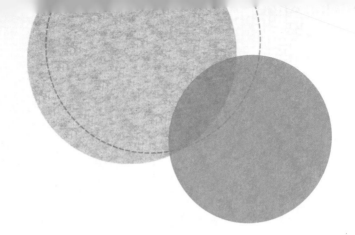

Art Director: Chris Opheim
Editor: Theresa Trinder
Designer: Laura Elsenraat
Production Designer: Dan Horton

Published by Hallmark Gift Books,
A division of Hallmark Cards, Inc.,
Kansas City, MO 64141
Visit us on the Web at Hallmark.com.

ISBN: 978-1-59530-785-9
1BOK2226
Printed and bound in China.

NOW YOU'RE

60!

MILESTONES & MEMORIES FOR YOUR GENERATION

By Brandon M. Crose

Hallmark

> "FORGET THE BLOCK...
> WHEN YOU'RE SIXTY,
> YOU'VE BEEN AROUND THE ENTIRE
> NEIGHBORHOOD A FEW TIMES."
> —*Dane Peddigrew*

America's "TV Generation" has seen the most dramatic changes in politics and culture of any generation before or since. You were raised in a time of growth, prosperity, and the very real threat of nuclear annihilation. You came of age amidst war, protest, and revolutionary music. You remember a time before personal computers, where you were when JFK was shot, and your first color television. Most significantly, your story is the story of how much America has changed... and how much you have changed with it.

WHEN YOU WERE BORN...

IN THE NEWS

Your parents still liked Ike! After a spate of health problems, President Eisenhower barely campaigned for his second term and handily won over Adlai Stevenson— 36 million votes to 26 million.

"History is on our side. We will bury you!" Nikita Khrushchev assumed power in a Communist Soviet government, giving Americans little hope of a thaw in the ongoing Cold War.

Though you were way too young to apply for an account, perhaps your parents had one of the very first credit cards, The Diner's Club, available in the early 1950s. (It was made out of cardboard, unfortunately, until the ever-popular plastic versions were manufactured about ten years later.)

There were only forty-eight states until Alaska and Hawaii became the forty-ninth and fiftieth. (But your parents were probably more eager to vacation in one of them over the other…)

WHEN YOU WERE BORN

EVENTS

At the height of the polio epidemic in America—
more than 57,628 new cases were reported in a single
year—Jonas Salk finally introduced a successful
vaccine. The crippling disease, which had affected
mostly children but sometimes adults, would become
almost nonexistent within the decade.

Scientific advancements seemed to belong more to
science fiction than reality: Sputnik I and then II circled
Earth, America and the Soviet Union both successfully
tested intercontinental ballistic missiles, and an early
test of the hydrogen bomb at Bikini Atoll was estimat-
ed to burn five times hotter than the sun's core.

As the long-term consequences of exposure to even
small amounts of radiation became clear, 9,000
scientists from 50 countries asked the United Nations
to ban above-ground nuclear testing.

The world became a smaller place with the
invention of the jet engine. Pan American's jet
planes offered America's first commercial trans-
Atlantic flights: from New York to London.

WHEN YOU
WERE BORN

MUSIC

You may not remember now, but "The Ballad of Davy Crockett" by Fess Parker, "My Prayer" by The Platters, and "Banana Boat Song" by Harry Belafonte were likely among the first songs you ever heard.

Ray Charles found his breakout hit in "I Got a Woman" (also covered by The King on his self-titled debut album *Elvis Presley*) and continued to crank out R&B chart toppers, such as "This Little Girl of Mine," "Lonely Avenue," "Drown in My Own Tears," "The Night Time (Is the Right Time)," and "A Fool For You."

Released under his stage name David Seville, Ross Bagdasarian's hit Christmas record "The Chipmunk Song (Christmas Don't Be Late)" featured the first appearance of Alvin and the Chipmunks.

WHEN YOU
WERE BORN

A young Elvis Presley soared to the top of the charts and stayed there with rock 'n' roll hits "Heartbreak Hotel," "Hound Dog," "Don't Be Cruel," "All Shook Up," and "Love Me Tender."

NOW SHOWING:

TO CATCH A THIEF

REBEL WITHOUT A CAUSE

OLD YELLER

MOVIES

Alfred Hitchcock was the undisputed Master of Suspense with hit movies *To Catch a Thief, Vertigo,* and *North by Northwest.*

> James Dean, icon of teenage rebellion, made only three movies—*East of Eden, Rebel Without a Cause,* and *Giant* (released posthumously)—before his untimely death at the age of 24.

The New York Times called *Old Yeller* "a warm, appealing little rustic tale," but if you later saw it as a child you probably never forgot its heart-wrenching climax.

The silver screen (and box office) stars of the time included James Stewart, Grace Kelly, John Wayne, Marilyn Monroe, Marlon Brando, Kim Novak, William Holden, Humphrey Bogart, and Clark Gable.

WHEN YOU WERE BORN

TV

By the mid '50s, Americans were buying an average of seven million TV sets per year. Approximately one in seven American families owned at least one television, and the typical viewer spent 42 hours per week watching it.

Some of the hit shows your parents spent all those hours watching may have included *I Love Lucy, The Ed Sullivan Show, Gunsmoke, The Jack Benny Show, Dragnet, General Electric Theater, You Bet Your Life,* and *The $64,000 Question.*

Your parents were also likely among the 30 million viewers to watch the wedding of celebrity actress Grace Kelly to Prince Rainier III of Monaco.

The original "Man of Steel" was not Christopher Reeve, but George Reeves, in *Adventures of Superman.* His costume was brown and gray until the show was later broadcast in color.

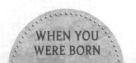

WHEN YOU
WERE BORN

SEPTEMBER 19, 1955

SPORTS
ILLUSTRATED

ROCKY THE CHAMP

IN THIS ISSUE:
HOW ARCHIE
PLANS TO BEAT HIM

25 CENTS
$7.50 A YEAR

Mickey Mantle's hallowed Triple Crown season included .340 batting and 52 home runs, helping the Yankees clinch the pennant against the Dodgers.

**Heavyweight champion
Rocky "The Rock" Marciano
retired from boxing at the age of 31,
undefeated. He won forty-nine fights;
all but six of them ended in a KO.**

Jim Brown debuted with the Cleveland Browns, leading the league in his first year with 942 yards rushing (including a record-breaking 237 in one game against the Los Angeles Rams).

New York baseball fans lost not one but two teams when longtime rivals the New York Giants and the Brooklyn Dodgers both moved to California.

WHEN YOU
WERE BORN

POP CULTURE

Parents were most likely to name their baby boys Michael, David, James, Robert, or John. For baby girls, Mary, Deborah, Susan, Linda, and Debra were the most popular choices.

Suburbia! Housing developments were everywhere—during 1957, for instance, a new home was built every seven seconds. Despite the sudden recession, the American Dream of home ownership was within reach.

Many young families lived in suburban developments such as Levittown, a community of 17,000 nearly identical homes, where, as agreed upon on by contract, grass had to be cut once a week and laundry hung only on rotary racks.

Your family may have had a fallout shelter in your basement or backyard for fear of a nuclear attack on American soil. The government encouraged this precaution, circulating pamphlets like "Six Steps to Survival" and "Facts about Fallout."

WHEN YOU WERE BORN

WHEN YOU WERE A KID...

The public assassination of President John F. Kennedy became the defining moment of your generation. For many, it was the end of an era marked by innocence and optimism.

Lyndon B. Johnson (or "LBJ") won a landslide victory over opponent Barry Goldwater—43 million to 27 million votes—remaining in the office he inherited from JFK.

The nation mourned the loss of several political and civil rights leaders: Robert F. Kennedy, Martin Luther King, Jr., and Malcolm X were all assassinated within a tumultuous three-year span.

Whether you served or knew someone who did, you were touched in some way by the war in Vietnam. Nearly nine million served from 1964 to 1973, during which time over 58,000 Americans were killed and over 300,000 were wounded.

EVENTS

Congress passed the Civil Rights Act, banning segregation in public places and employment discrimination on the basis of race, color, religion, sex, or national origin. President Lyndon B. Johnson signed the Act with more than 75 pens—which he later bestowed upon congressional supporters and civil rights leaders, such as Hubert Humphrey and Martin Luther King, Jr.

In pursuit of his "Great Society," President Lyndon Johnson passed even more landmark legislation, this time to reduce poverty, create affordable housing, protect the environment, provide government health insurance for the sick and elderly, and set standards for the quality of drinking water.

If your parents purchased a new car after 1966, it came equipped with seat beats (in all seats) and shatter-resistant windshields. Consumer advocate Ralph Nader's book *Unsafe at Any Speed* played a large part in making these safety standards law.

The birth control pill gave women the ability to plan or prevent pregnancy, and the Baby Boom came to an end.

WHEN YOU
WERE A KID

MUSIC

You couldn't have missed The Beatles—they already had the top five spots on the Billboard Hot 100 singles chart before their first-ever American appearance on *The Ed Sullivan Show.*

If you loved The Jackson 5, you were not alone. "I Want You Back," "ABC," "The Love You Save," and "I'll Be There" all hit the top of the charts less than a year after the group's debut. Stickers, posters, sew-on patches, and coloring books soon followed—there was even a Saturday morning cartoon on ABC called *Jackson 5ive.*

The Monkees, a fictional TV band modeled after the early years of The Beatles, had several hit songs, including "Last Train to Clarksville," "I'm a Believer," and "A Little Bit Me, A Little Bit You."

Some of your other favorite songs might have included "Chim Chim Cher-ee" from the movie *Mary Poppins,* "The Sounds of Silence" by Simon & Garfunkel, and "Monday, Monday" by The Mamas & the Papas.

WHEN YOU WERE A KID

MOVIES

Some of the most memorable movies of your childhood years were musicals: *My Fair Lady, A Hard Day's Night,* and *Viva Las Vegas* all hit theaters in the same year.

Speaking of musicals, you may have wanted to be a singing, dancing von Trapp child after seeing *The Sound of Music* for the first time.

Walt Disney—creator (and voice) of Mickey Mouse, pioneer of the feature-length cartoon, and founder of an entertainment empire—died from lung cancer at the age of 65. (Despite persistent rumors that his body was cryonically preserved, his remains were cremated.)

Your childhood was not without Disney, however—Roy Disney (Walt's older brother) kept the company moving forward. You may have seen the Disney classic *The Jungle Book* when it was first in theaters.

WHEN YOU WERE A KID

NOW SHOWING:

THE SOUND OF MUSIC

A HARD DAY'S NIGHT

VIVA LAS VEGAS

TV

....

Many television firsts played a large role in John F. Kennedy's short presidency. You saw the first-ever televised presidential debate, which gave the more "telegenic" Kennedy a distinct advantage over Richard Nixon. You saw President Kennedy give the first live televised press conference. And JFK's assassination was covered in a level of detail like never before over the course of four days, which even included the first televised murder—that of Lee Harvey Oswald as he was being transferred to the Dallas county jail.

But it wasn't all bad—you had great shows like *Batman, Lassie, Flipper, The Munsters, Captain Kangaroo, The Addams Family,* and *Gilligan's Island*.

And if your parents let you watch it, you may have seen the last episode of *The Fugitive* (along with 25 million other households).

WHEN YOU
WERE A KID

WHILE IT ONLY LASTED THREE
SEASONS, THE ORIGINAL *STAR TREK*
SERIES' DIVERSE CREW HAD A MAJOR
IMPACT ON POPULAR CULTURE—
AND "TREKKIES" WOULD BE ABLE
TO TUNE IN LATER TO ONE OF FOUR
SPIN-OFF TV SERIES.

You knew world heavyweight champion Cassius Clay to be brash and unpredictable. Still, many boxing fans were stunned when the world heavyweight champion converted to Islam and changed his name to "Muhammad Ali."

As more and more families began purchasing color TV sets and fans could finally see the color of their team's uniforms, the popularity of Sunday football soared. The Super Bowl was created to give this growing audience something to cheer for.

Did you play tennis with a one-handed backhand? Billie Jean King's reign as the top women's tennis player may be responsible for that.

Perhaps you believed that "Winning isn't everything; it's the only thing"? It worked for Vince Lombardi— he coached the Green Bay Packers to a third straight NFL Championship.

WHEN YOU WERE A KID

POP CULTURE

It was a great time to be a kid: the Spirograph hit stores, everyone owned a Frisbee, and breakfast became a lot sweeter, thanks to new brands like Pop-Tarts, Lucky Charms, and Cap'n Crunch!

Barbie got a younger sister, Skipper, and your first G.I. Joe was nearly a foot tall, with twenty-one moving parts and a plethora of optional costumes and accessories.

Not everything was new—old classics such as Tinkertoys, Lincoln Logs, and Erector Sets were just as popular during your childhood as in your parents'.

For a special treat (and a night off from cooking for Mom), everyone piled into the family's station wagon for dinner at the nearby drive-in restaurant: the local Dog n Suds, Sonic, A&W, or Sandy's—depending on where you lived.

WHEN YOU
WERE A KID

WHEN YOU WERE A TEENAGER...

IN THE NEWS

Richard Nixon became the first-ever American president to visit the People's Republic of China. Later, he also became the first president to visit the USSR when he met with Soviet leaders in Moscow.

Like many Americans, your confidence in the U.S. government may have been shaken when President Nixon then became the first—and only—president to ever resign (rather than be impeached over the break-in at the Watergate hotel).

People tied yellow ribbons around trees to celebrate a cease-fire agreement in the Vietnam War, though America was the only nation to honor the treaty.

After a 121-day trial, Charles Manson and three members of his cult were sentenced to death for the brutal murder of actress Sharon Tate and four others. (Their sentences became "life in prison" when the death penalty was suspended a year later.)

WHEN YOU
WERE A TEEN

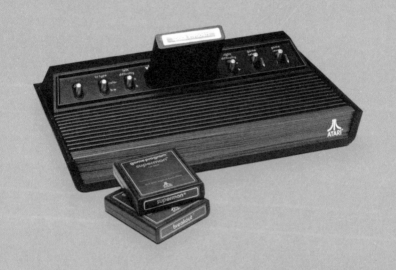

It was a time of great change for both our physical and social environments. Growing national interest paved the way for the Clean Air and Clean Water Acts, the Supreme Court ruled it unconstitutional to deny women an abortion within the first trimester of pregnancy, and the American Psychiatric Association removed homosexuality from its list of mental disorders.

You may not have known it at the time, but you witnessed the dawn of the video game with Pong. Modeled after table tennis, this deceptively simple game made its creators very wealthy…and paved the way for Atari's many home consoles and games.

Technology seemed to be growing at an unchecked rate: doctors could now see your brain with a CAT scan and, just several years after the first man walked on the moon, and a space station called "Skylab" was orbiting the Earth.

An oil embargo caused soaring prices, long lines at the gas station, and a federally mandated speed limit of 55 MPH. Japanese economy cars—such as the Nissan Datsun, which boasted 30 miles per gallon (when the national average was 13.5)—became very popular.

WHEN YOU WERE A TEEN

MUSIC

Rock 'n' roll had evolved—and not quietly. Heavy metal bands Led Zeppelin, AC/DC, Aerosmith, and Van Halen blew out their amps (and your parents' eardrums); punk rockers The Sex Pistols, Patti Smith, The Velvet Underground, and The Ramones spoke directly to your teenaged rebellion; and innovative rockers The Eagles and Fleetwood Mac changed the musical landscape.

Fascinated or repulsed, it was impossible not to react to your first sighting of the androgynous space creature with glittery clothing and orange hair. David Bowie personified "Glam Rock" as Ziggy Stardust.

You were probably too young for Woodstock, but you couldn't have missed the short-lived Disco Era. The craze began with the Hues Corporation's hit "Rock the Boat."

Other hit songs often heard on your radio (or perhaps your first car's 8-track tape player) included Elton John's "Rocket Man," Carly Simon's "You're So Vain," and Barbra Streisand's "The Way We Were."

WHEN YOU WERE A TEEN

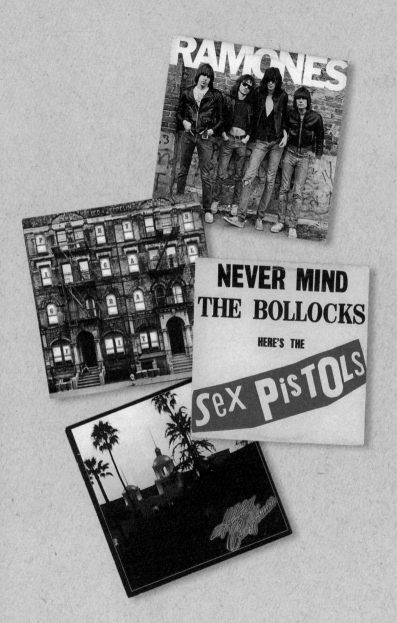

MOVIES

The memorable movies of your teenage years are still classics today: *The Godfather, Caberet, American Graffiti, Chinatown, Blazing Saddles, One Flew over the Cuckoo's Nest,* and one film that made you think twice about a day at the beach: *Jaws.*

Last Tango in Paris portrayed Marlon Brando in a new light—it was the first X-rated film to feature a major Hollywood star.

You probably couldn't look at pea soup the same way again after seeing *The Exorcist.* Arguably the most terrifying horror movie ever made, its grotesque special effects actually caused heart attacks in some theaters.

Whether for pure escapist fun or fear of an uncertain future, disaster movies like *The Poseidon Adventure* and *Earthquake* were big hits.

WHEN YOU
WERE A TEEN

Your black and white television set did not mean that you were completely behind the times—by the early '70s, only half of America watched television in color. Either way you watched it, you probably tuned into a documentary called *The Selling of the Pentagon* . . . or any of the 250 hours of the Senate Watergate hearings.

> **Rowan and Martin's Laugh-In redefined television sketch show comedy and gave you and your friends catchy phrases like "Sock it to me," "Here come de judge," and "You bet your sweet bippy."**

Based on the hit movie of the same name, the television series *M*A*S*H* told the story of an army hospital's staff who tried to find humor amidst the grim reality of the Korean War. Though it premiered to low ratings, the show would last for eleven years.

Other popular shows of your teen years included *All in the Family, Sanford and Son, The Mary Tyler Moore Show, Hawaii Five-O, The Beverly Hillbillies, Green Acres,* and *Bonanza.*

SPORTS

● ●

The world watched in horror as Palestinian terrorists held hostage—and killed—eleven Israeli athletes at the Munich Olympics.

Billie Jean King scored a victory for women everywhere (and female athletes in particular) when she humbled Bobby Riggs in an exhibition tennis match billed as the "Battle of the Sexes."

Hank Aaron beat Babe Ruth's home run record of 714. And he didn't stop there—Aaron holds a total of 755 career home runs. In his own words: "I don't want them to forget Ruth; I just want them to remember me!"

Try as you might, you will probably never forget football personality Joe Namath wearing pantyhose for a Hanes Beautymist commercial.

WHEN YOU
WERE A TEEN

POP CULTURE

Men had long hair and mustaches, women wore maxi dresses or mini skirts with knee socks, love beads were boss, mood rings were far out, and maybe you didn't have a cat or a dog, but you probably did have a Pet Rock.

Your first car may have been a brand new Volkswagon "Super" Beetle, Oldsmobile Omega, or Chevrolet Corvette, but more likely your father gave you his old car—perhaps a 1964 Ford Country Squire?

If you exchanged vows right out of high school, you faced some sobering statistics—the divorce rate had doubled since 1966.

Health foods were a fad, but the number of fast food restaurants doubled over the course of several years—from 3,400 in 1967 to almost 7,000 in 1972. Most people ate one-third of their meals out of the house.

WHEN YOU
WERE A TEEN

WHEN YOU WERE IN YOUR 20s...

IN THE NEWS

You and many others watched, helpless, as Iran militants seized sixty-six American citizens and held most of them hostage at a U.S. embassy in Tehran for over a year.

A partial meltdown at a nuclear power plant less than ten miles from Harrisburg, Pennsylvania (and one-hundred miles from Washington, D.C.) caused nationwide panic. Three Mile Island is now cited as the worst nuclear accident in American history.

"Where were you when the mountain blew?" Hopefully nowhere near it. Mt. St. Helens erupted with a force greater than 500 atomic bombs, killing 57 people and sending a drifting 16-mile-high plume of ash as far as Idaho and Montana.

Many Americans decided that they were not, in fact, better off than they were four years ago, and Ronald Reagan won the presidential election over incumbent Jimmy Carter in a historic landslide. The Reagan Revolution promised to restore "the great, confident roar of American progress and growth and optimism." And for many, it did.

IN YOUR 20s

You were shocked by the assassination attempt on President Ronald Reagan, only 69 days in office, by John Hinckley, Jr.—and perhaps shocked again when the president returned to work a mere three days after a bullet had pierced his lung.

While the rest of the country suffered from an energy crisis and deep recession, a growing technology boom (not to mention the nice weather) convinced many to relocate to the South and Southwest—these states saw a population increase of more than 25%!

Perhaps you owned one of the first Apple II computer systems? Soon after its debut, personal computers could be found in many homes. *Time* magazine even revised their "Man of the Year" feature to award the personal computer with "Machine of the Year."

Gender equality scored another victory when Arizona judge Sandra Day O'Connor became the first female U.S. Supreme Court Justice.

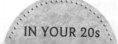

IN YOUR 20s

MUSIC

Five years after The King of Rock 'n' Roll passed away, Michael Jackson revitalized the genre with his sophomore album *Thriller*, which earned Jackson a record eight Grammy awards. (And, if you had $900–$1,000 to burn, you may have listened to *Thriller* on the Sony CDP-101—the world's first commercially released CD player.)

Madonna's self-titled debut album included five hit singles, though the "Material Girl" drew controversy for her explicit lyrics and music videos.

Think the title track to Bruce Springsteen's hit album "Born in the USA" is about American pride? Many did, and still do. However, "The Boss" wrote the song about how shamefully Vietnam veterans were treated after the war ended.

It was a popular time for music to "give back," as "We Are the World" was recorded in Los Angeles, the "Live Aid" concert raised money for African famine relief, and "Farm Aid" raised funds and awareness for American family farmers.

IN YOUR 20s

NOW SHOWING:

E.T.

RAIDERS OF THE LOST ARK

RETURN OF THE JEDI

MOVIES

Blockbuster popcorn flicks reigned supreme: you probably saw *Raiders of the Lost Ark, Return of the Jedi, Ghostbusters, The Terminator,* and *Back to the Future* in the theater. Perhaps several times.

The most popular movie of the decade, however, was about a little alien who wanted to "phone home." *E.T., the Extra-Terrestrial* **sold close to 142 million tickets.**

Burt Reynolds, Jane Fonda, John Travolta, Sally Field, Clint Eastwood, Sissy Spacek, Harrison Ford, Barbra Streisand, Dustin Hoffman, and Goldie Hawn were the leading stars of the day.

"Movie night" didn't always mean going to the theater— now all you had to do was rent a VHS tape from your local video rental store and pop it into your VCR. (Let's hope you didn't forget to rewind!)

IN YOUR 20s

TV

You grew up with only three to five channels, but now there are almost 60! More and more American homes were subscribing to cable TV. (Though some came to agree with Bruce Springsteen: "There's 57 channels and nothing on!")

Now you could watch your music, too! Sales of videocassette tapes soared with the launch of MTV, the first 24-hour music video network.

Why go to the mall? The Home Shopping Network gave you the ability to make all of your impulse purchases from the comfort of your home.

The final episode of *M*A*S*H* shattered TV records by drawing 105.97 million viewers. It held this record for 27 years—until 2010's *Super Bowl XLIV*.

IN YOUR 20s

SPORTS

If you don't remember much about the 1980 Summer Olympics in Moscow, that's probably because *we* weren't there. Led by President Jimmy Carter, America and more than 60 other nations boycotted the games in protest of Soviet military action in Afghanistan.

However, you couldn't have missed that same year's Winter Olympics. Hosted in Lake Placid, New York, the U.S. men's ice hockey team scored a miraculous "Cold War" victory over the much more experienced Soviet team, even going on to win the gold medal.

Major League Baseball players went on strike over the issue of free-agent compensation. The strike lasted 49 days, resulting in the cancellation of 713 games.

The American star of the 1984 Olympic Games in Los Angeles was track-and-field athlete Carl Lewis, who took four gold medals.

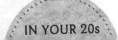

IN YOUR 20s

POP CULTURE

Were you a "Yuppie"? It was a good time to be one: "young urban professionals" saw great profit from the deregulation of big businesses. Many forgot "peace, love, and happiness" in favor of a new credo: "Money is power."

It's all about you! Self-help books, from *Richard Simmons' Never-Say-Diet Book* to *You Can Negotiate Anything,* began to fly off the shelves.

Two instant classics joined the "funnies" section of your newspaper: Gary Larson's "The Far Side" and Greg Howard's "Sally Forth."

If you had boys, you were most likely to name them Michael, Christopher, Jason, Matthew, or David. If you had girls, you were likely to name them Jennifer, Melissa, Jessica, Amanda, or Sarah.

IN YOUR 20s

Leisure suits were falling out of favor, but by the time you entered the workforce, business attire had indeed become more casual: sleeveless sweaters, print shirts, patterned jackets, and ties were the norm.

WHEN YOU WERE IN YOUR 30s...

IN THE NEWS

The Exxon Valdez, piloted by an inexperienced third mate, went off course and struck a reef in Alaska's Prince William Sound, spreading more than 11 million gallons of crude oil over 1,300 miles of pristine coastline.

You might have had to do "duck and cover" drills in school, but your kids wouldn't have to. The Cold War came to a symbolic end with the fall of the Berlin Wall.

"Today the majority of South Africans, black and white, recognize that apartheid has no future." After 27 years in prison for resisting a government that valued white lives over black, Nelson Mandela was free to continue his efforts to abolish apartheid.

Still reeling from race riots after the Rodney King trial just two years earlier, Los Angeles was rocked by an early morning earthquake measuring 6.6 on the Richter scale.

All 51 days televised, the standoff between followers of David Koresh and federal agents at a Waco, Texas, compound ended with the deaths of over eighty people.

IN YOUR 30s

EVENTS

Arguably the most important dinosaur discovery of all time, the most complete Tyrannosaurus Rex skeleton was found after only 65 million years near Faith, South Dakota. "Sue" (named after the person who found her) rests her bones in Chicago's Field Museum.

Meanwhile, scientific advancements continued to bring you closer to science fiction: lasers were approved to perform precise eye surgery, your telephone went cordless, and you may have learned about black holes from Stephen Hawking's best-selling book *A Brief History of Time*.

You may have installed an extra phone line to check e-mail and surf the Web without fear of being "booted" whenever someone needed to use the phone. Full-service programs like Prodigy, CompuServe, or America Online offered an easy way to keep in touch.

Genetic modification allowed farmers to begin growing produce that was larger and more resistant to insecticides, though some scientists worried about the effects that these altered crops could have on the environment.

IN YOUR 30s

A familiar band reunited to release a best-selling live album: The Eagles' *Hell Freezes Over* debuted at number one on the charts.

MUSIC

Eric Clapton's hit song "Tears in Heaven" had a somber backstory—the loss of his four-year-old son. The heart-felt ballad resonated with many, and also earned three Grammy Awards.

Whitney Houston made her big screen debut with Kevin Costner in *The Bodyguard*, and the album (which featured her international chart-topping cover of Dolly Parton's "I Will Always Love You") became the best-selling soundtrack of all time.

Other familiar hit songs include Bette Middler's "Wind Beneath My Wings," Roxette's "It Must Have Been Love," and Paula Abdul's "Rush Rush."

IN YOUR 30s

MOVIES

You may have thought about taking pottery lessons after seeing Patrick Swayze and Demi Moore's famous love scene in *Ghost*.

Everything old was new again. Hit movies based on the television shows of your youth included *The Addams Family* and *The Fugitive*.

Forrest Gump gave a new perspective to the memorable events you experienced first-hand and introduced his philosophy, "Life is like a box of chocolates."

You probably also enjoyed *Thelma and Louise*, *The Piano*, and the heartrending *Schindler's List*, which earned a staggering twelve Academy Award nominations and six actual awards, including Best Director and Best Picture.

IN YOUR 30s

NOW SHOWING:

GHOST

FORREST GUMP

THELMA AND LOUISE

You may have identified with *Thirtysomething*'s Baby Boomers as they navigated the trials of having children and growing older, while *The Cosby Show* was an unparalleled family hit.

"Heeeeeeeere's Johnny!" After thirty years of being the gold standard in late-night television, you watched Johnny Carson's tearful farewell to *The Tonight Show*.

You may have been one of the millions who stayed up late to watch the O.J. Simpson police chase. Every minute of the subsequent trial was also aired live— and watched by millions.

Nearly 60% of Americans spent most evenings on the couch, giving rise to the term "couch potato."

While on that couch, many potatoes enjoyed hit shows like *America's Funniest Home Videos*, *Cheers*, *Designing Women*, *Murphy Brown*, *Roseanne*, *Home Improvement*, and *Unsolved Mysteries*.

IN YOUR 30s

SPORTS

Cincinnati Reds batter Pete Rose, after surpassing 4,191 hits to break a record set 57 years earlier by Ty Cobb, was ousted from baseball as a result of his illegal betting.

Baseball fans were not pleased when a 257-day strike led to the cancellation of that year's World Series.

Twenty years after losing the World Heavyweight Title to Muhammad Ali (and after ten years away from heavyweight competitions), George Foreman reclaimed his title by knocking out Michael Moorer in ten rounds.

**Three-time MVP Lakers player
Earvin "Magic" Johnson, Jr. held
an emotional press conference,
announcing that he had tested positive
for HIV, putting a new face
on the AIDS epidemic.**

IN YOUR 30s

The private lives of celebrities were suddenly matters of great interest. Supermarket tabloids—such as *Star*, *The Globe*, and *The National Enquirer*—sold by the tens of millions.

Casual yet durable clothes by L.L.Bean and Eddie Bauer were in, and if your company was one of many that now offered Dress-Down Days, you could even wear them to work!

Dr. Deepak Chopra may have changed your mind about Alternative Medicine with his best-selling book *Ageless Body, Timeless Mind*. If so, you weren't alone— *Time* magazine even named Chopra one of the Top 100 Icons and Heroes of the Century.

Plastic flowers danced to music, fanny packs were hip, books on tape let you read while driving, the much-disliked New Coke was replaced with Coca-Cola Classic, highly collectible Beanie Babies were *definitely* going to be worth a lot of money someday, and you learned that *Men Are from Mars, Women Are from Venus*.

WHEN YOU WERE IN YOUR 40s...

IN THE NEWS

September 11th, 2001. We will never forget.

You'd witnessed the Challenger explosion, and you were saddened to see the second major disaster in the history of the space shuttle program as the space shuttle Columbia unexpectedly disintegrated after its return from a successful 16-day mission. All seven astronauts were killed, and the nation mourned…again.

From Mr. Universe, to the Terminator, to…California's 38th Governor? After surprising the world by announcing his candidacy on *The Tonight Show with Jay Leno*, voters elected Arnold Schwarzenegger over 134 other candidates.

No one expected the devastation of Hurricane Katrina. The Category Four storm claimed the lives of nearly 2,000 New Orleans natives…and the homes of many, many more.

IN YOUR 40s

Y2K

EVENTS

Just as it seemed you were living in the modern world that had been promised to you as a child, the Y2K Bug threatened to send society back to the 1900s by exploiting an oversight in computers' internal clocks.

Predicted to revolutionize transportation as we know it, the Segway debuted on the consumer market for a mere $4,950.

Were you one of 50 million people without power during the Northeast Blackout of 2003? After a cascading power failure, eight U.S. states and parts of Canada were left without electricity for a day or longer.

A massive earthquake measuring 9.0 on the Richter scale loosed a disastrous tsunami on Southeast Asia, killing over 225,000 and displacing 1.2 million more.

MUSIC

> You listened to your music on LPs,
> 8-tracks, cassette tapes, and CDs...
> and then MP3 devices promised to
> contain your entire music library!

American Idol launched the careers of talented performers Kelly Clarkson, Carrie Underwood, Chris Daughtry, and Jennifer Hudson. (As well as musical oddity William Hung.)

Alicia Keys was a piano-playing phenomenon, stacking up five Grammy awards for her debut album *Songs in A Minor,* including Best R&B Album, Song of the Year, and Best New Artist.

Other familiar hit songs from this time include the positive anthems "Believe" by Cher, "Breathe" by Faith Hill, and "Beautiful" by Christina Aguilera.

IN YOUR 40s

MOVIES

Thanks to her powerful performance in *Monster's Ball*, Halle Berry became the first African-American woman to win an Academy Award for "Best Actress."

George Lucas released the long-awaited prequel to the original Star Wars trilogy of your thirties—*Episode I: The Phantom Menace*. Despite its mixed reviews, it was by far the top grossing film of its year.

Whether you read the books when they were first published, or just remember seeing "Frodo Lives!" on buttons and t-shirts later on, no one would deny that Peter Jackson's massively epic (and epically massive) *Lord of the Rings* film trilogy was the movie event of the decade.

Other familiar movies from this time might include *The Sixth Sense, American Beauty, The Matrix, Gladiator, Almost Famous,* and *A Beautiful Mind.*

IN YOUR 40s

NOW SHOWING:

LORD OF THE RINGS

GLADIATOR

A BEAUTIFUL MIND

You had to spring for the premium cable package (or wait for the DVDs) to catch some of the best shows on television, such as *The Sopranos, Six Feet Under, The Wire, The Shield,* and *Battlestar Galactica.*

Mega-popular "Reality TV" shows such as *Survivor, America's Next Top Model,* and *Dancing with the Stars* began to eclipse scripted dramas and comedies.

"The truth is out there."
Spanning nine seasons, four lead actors,
and many, many conspiracy theories,
***The X-Files* aired its final episode.**

Other popular shows you watched may have included *Who Wants to Be a Millionaire?, ER, Friends, Frasier, Law & Order, Everybody Loves Raymond, C.S.I.: Crime Scene Investigation,* and *Will & Grace.*

IN YOUR 40s

SPORTS

The 2002 Winter Olympics were held in Salt Lake City, with the United States setting a record for winning the most gold and total medals at a home Winter Olympics, though Norway took home the most gold medals.

Michelle Kwan's clean programs and deep, quiet edges earned her numerous figure skating medals and championships, making her one of the most popular female athletes for over a decade.

Long-beleaguered Boston Red Sox fans had their day when their team beat the St. Louis Cardinals to win their first World Series Championship in eighty-six years. The "Curse of the Bambino" was at last reversed!

IN YOUR 40s

NASCAR fans were stunned when seven-time Winston Cup champion Dale Earnhardt suffered a fatal crash during the final lap of the Daytona 500.

POP CULTURE

Muggles of all ages made time to read about Harry Potter and his friends Ron and Hermione. J.K. Rowling's endearing books spawned several successful movies and a plethora of merchandise, but they were not loved by all—some schools banned the books for fear that they promoted witchcraft.

The death of Diana, Princess of Wales, may have introduced the word "paparazzi" into your life, as well as a renewed contempt for tabloid culture.

The book *Fast Food Nation* and, later, the documentary movie *Super Size Me* made many rethink what they ordered when they dined out.

Crocs were in, low-carb diets like Atkins were all the rage, young people were abuzz with energy drinks, and, after 9/11, it seemed that everyone had an American flag sticker on their car window or bumper.

WHEN YOU WERE IN YOUR 50s...

IN THE NEWS

US Airways Flight 1549 was struck by a flock of geese shortly after takeoff, and Captain Chesley B. "Sully" Sullenberger became a national hero after making a crash landing in the Hudson River. Incredibly, no lives were lost.

Haiti was hit by a magnitude-7 earthquake, devastating the small Caribbean country and displacing 1.5 million people from their homes.

Iceland's Eyjafjallajökull volcano erupted for the first time since 1821, sending a plume of volcanic ash 30,000 feet into the air and grounding airplanes from the United Kingdom to Russia for six days.

Almost 23 million Americans watched the royal wedding ceremony of Prince William and Kate Middleton, Duchess of Cambridge, at Westminster Abbey in London.

Following an international manhunt lasting almost ten years and two presidencies, U.S. military forces at last found Osama bin Laden, architect of the 9/11 attacks.

IN YOUR 50s

EVENTS

· ·

**From humble beginnings to
44th President of the United States,
Barack Obama showed the world that
the American dream is very much alive.**

Previously a bulky thing for affluent people (or show-offs), the cell phone evolved by leaps and bounds. Suddenly everyone had one—and the home phone (or "landline") became, for many, an obsolete expense.

The "Great Recession," which began with the collapse of AIG, Lehman Brothers, and Bear Sterns, likely made it difficult for your children to find a job or buy a house.

Despite popular fears that it could create a black hole in the middle of Western Europe, the Large Hadron Collider resumed operations, accelerating particles to previously unseen speeds in an attempt to learn more about the origins of our universe.

IN YOUR 50s

MOVIES

Superhero movies, many featuring characters that first debuted in comic books you may have owned, were everywhere! (And, by the way, if you still own those comic books they're probably worth a few dollars…)

Kathryn Bigelow became the first woman to win Best Director at the Academy Awards for *The Hurt Locker*, which depicted the story of a bomb-disposal team during the Iraq War.

A French black-and-white silent film, *The Artist*, was nominated for ten Oscars and took home five, including Best Picture, Best Director, and Best Actor.

You may have also enjoyed *The Blind Side*, *Up in the Air*, *The Town*, *Midnight in Paris*, *The Fighter*, *Tinker Tailor Soldier Spy*, *The Help*, *My Week with Marilyn*, or *The King's Speech*.

IN YOUR 50s

MUSIC

The world was stunned to learn that Michael Jackson died of a drug overdose less than a month before his sold-out concerts in London. Grieving fans bought 35 million of his albums, making Jackson the best-selling artist of 2009.

The title track from Lady Antebellum's second album, *Need You Now*, was a big hit and introduced the Nashville trio to those who might not usually listen to country music. They took home both Song of the Year and Album of the Year at the 2011 Grammy Awards.

With the option to buy your music online by the song or album, digital downloads eclipsed sales of the physical CD.

Some hit songs you might have downloaded included "Poker Face" by Lady Gaga, "Firework" by Katy Perry, and "Hey, Soul Sister" by Train.

IN YOUR 50s

"BABY, YOU'RE A FIREWORK
COME ON, LET YOUR COLORS BURST
MAKE 'EM GO, "AAH, AAH, AAH"
YOU'RE GONNA LEAVE 'EM ALL IN
AWE, AWE, AWE..."

Katy Perry—*Firework*, 2010

· ·

Remember when the first television sets were built into really heavy wooden cabinets? Most flat screen TVs are so light that they can be mounted on your wall.

One particular show was certain to bring back some memories. It was *Mad Men*—a period drama about the people who work at a New York advertising firm during the 1960s.

Music isn't the only thing that's gone digital—now you can watch TV shows on your computer, too.

In fact, you probably heard that more and more people were canceling their expensive cable packages in favor of online streaming services like Netflix, Hulu, and Amazon Prime. Maybe you were one of them.

IN YOUR 50s

SPORTS

A long-delayed plan twenty years in the making, New York City finally opened two new ballparks in the same year—the New Yankee Stadium and Citi Field for the New York Yankees and the New York Mets, respectively.

The United States broke the record for the most medals won at a single Winter Olympics in 2010, with Americans Bode Miller and Shaun White having memorable breakout performances.

Tennis fans witnessed the longest match in tennis history as American John Isner played Nicolas Mahut of France at the Wimbledon Championships over the course of three days, for a total of 11 hours and 5 minutes.

Led by the "Big Three"—LeBron James, Chris Bosh, and Dwyane Wade—the Miami Heat won two NBA Finals against the Oklahoma City Thunder and then the San Antonio Spurs.

IN YOUR 50s

POP CULTURE

**You probably use popular
social networks such as Facebook
to keep in touch; half of all
"Boomers" maintain an online profile.**

You have likely discovered the Internet phenomenon that is YouTube—endless hours of homemade hilarity, officially licensed music videos, and some other things you probably wish you could forget.

Perhaps you have wondered why celebrities your age are starting to look younger than you do? In many cases, the answer is Botox injections, which temporarily paralyze certain facial muscles, smoothing wrinkles and creating a more youthful (if somewhat puffy) face.

If your children have had children of their own, your grandson(s) might be named Jacob, Michael, Joshua, Ethan, or Matthew. Your granddaughter(s) might be named Emily, Emma, Isabella, Madison, or Ava— some of the most popular baby names of the time.

IN YOUR 50s

NOW YOU'RE 60!

And you're in good company!
Look who else is in their 60s:

- Oprah Winfrey,
  talk show host and philanthropist
- Bill Gates, business magnate
- Meryl Streep, actress
- Sugar Ray Leonard, boxer
- Eddie Van Halen, musician
- Christie Brinkley, supermodel
- Tommy Hilfiger, clothing designer
- Al Franken, comedian and U.S. senator
- Condoleeza Rice, diplomat
- Bill Nye, scientist and TV personality
- George Strait, musician
- Arianna Huffington, journalist
- Lou Ferrigno, bodybuilder and actor

"You are not turning 60.
You are only turning 20
for the third time."

—*Anonymous*

"A diplomat is a man who
always remembers a woman's birthday
but never remembers her age."

—*Robert Frost*

"I'm sixty years of age.
That's 16 Celsius."

—*George Carlin*

DID YOU ENJOY THIS BOOK?

We would love to hear from you.

Please send your comments to:
Hallmark Book Feedback
P.O. Box 419034
Mail Drop 100
Kansas City, MO 64141

Or e-mail us at:
booknotes@hallmark.com